Wally Amos

Jeri Cipriano

Boston, Massachusetts
Chandler, Arizona
Glenview, Illinois
Upper Saddle River, New Jersey

Illustrations
2, 3, 5, 6, 8, 9, 11, 12, 14 Roger Stewart.

Photographs
Every effort has been made to secure permission and provide appropriate credit for photographic material.
The publisher deeply regrets any omission and pledges to correct errors called to its attention in subsequent editions.

Unless otherwise acknowledged, all photographs are the property of Pearson Education, Inc.

Photo locators denoted as follows: Top (T), Center (C), Bottom (B), Left (L), Right (R), Background (Bkgd)

Opener: Dana Edmunds, courtesy of Wally Amos; 1 Dana Edmunds, courtesy of Wally Amos; 4 Comstock Images/
Thinkstock; 7 Library of Congress; 10 kgelster/iStockphoto; 15 Dana Edmunds, courtesy of Wally Amos.

ISBN-13: 978-0-328-67620-0
ISBN-10: 0-328-67620-9

10 11 12 13 V0SI 18 17 16 15

Wally Amos always worked hard and tried new things. In 1975, he started a company called Famous Amos. He sold tasty chocolate chip cookies. People gobbled them up. What was his secret? It was Amos himself. He liked people, and they liked him.

Wally Amos was born in Florida in 1936. Amos learned good **manners** from his parents. He also learned to work hard. These lessons helped him later in life.

Young Amos wanted to make money. He cleaned people's shoes. He delivered newspapers. Amos had a **reputation** for being a good worker.

Amos also helped his mother. She cooked and sold food. Amos delivered the food.

Customers liked talking to Amos. He was polite and friendly to them. They gave him **tips**.

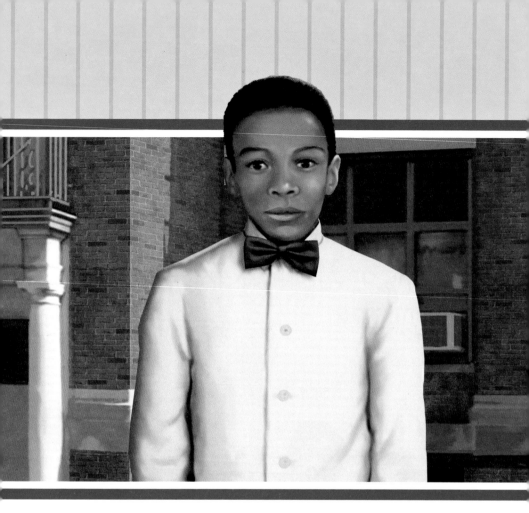

Each day, Amos walked eight miles to and from school. He went to a school for African American children. At this time, black and white children could not go to the same school. Amos thought this was unfair.

Amos's parents divorced when he was twelve. His mother sent him to New York City. He lived with his Aunt Della.

Aunt Della loved Amos. She made him chocolate chip cookies. They were very tasty.

Amos tried different jobs in New York. He tried becoming a cook. When he was older, he joined the Air Force. He also worked at a clothing store. None of these seemed right to him.

Amos got married and had children. He needed money to support them. He got a job working with famous singers. He helped them get jobs and make records. Some became his good friends.

Later, Amos moved to California.
He wanted to try something new.
He had good memories of Aunt Della.
He wanted to make a business
selling cookies.

Some of Amos's famous friends helped him. They gave him money to start a business. In 1975 he opened a store. It was called the Famous Amos Chocolate Chip Cookie store. Amos's picture was on every bag of cookies he sold.

To sell cookies, Amos went on television. He did interviews. He was in a parade. He became famous—just like the name of his company said!

Amos was very successful. The company made millions of dollars.

Things changed. By the late 1980s, Amos's business was losing money. He had to sell it to another company.

In the 1990s, a new company bought Famous Amos Chocolate Chip Cookies. They hired Amos. He was back selling his cookies.

Amos did other things as he got older. He wrote books. He helped children learn to read. Now he donates some of his **profits** to help others.

Amos thinks people need to believe in themselves to succeed. "If it could happen to me, Wally Amos," he says, "then it can happen to you."

Glossary

manners polite way of behaving

profits the amount of money a business earns after all expenses have been paid

reputation the opinion people have of someone or something

tips small sums of money given for a service